Collins

Social Studies for Jamaica Grade 9

Workbook

Series Editor: Farah Christian

William Collins' dream of knowledge for all began with the publication of his first book in 1819.A self-educated mill worker, he not only enriched millions of lives, but also founded a flourishing publishing house. Today, staying true to this spirit, Collins books are packed with inspiration, innovation and practical expertise. They place you at the centre of a world of possibility and give you exactly what you need to explore it.

Collins. Freedom to teach.

Published by Collins
An imprint of HarperCollins*Publishers*
The News Building, 1 London Bridge Street, London, SE1 9GF, UK

HarperCollins*Publishers*
Macken House, 39/40 Mayor Street Upper, Dublin 1, D01 C9W8, Ireland

Browse the complete Collins Caribbean catalogue at
www.collins.co.uk/caribbeanschools

10 9 8 7 6 5 4 3 2 1

ISBN 978-0-00-841401-6

British Library Cataloguing in Publication Data
A catalogue record for this publication is available from the British Library.

Publisher: Dr Elaine Higgleton
Commissioning editor: Kate Wigley
In-house senior editor: Craig Balfour
Author: Nick Coates
Series editor: Farah Christian
Editorial project management: Oriel Square
Copyeditor: Andy Slater
Series designer: Kevin Robbins
Cover photo: LBSimms Photography/Shutterstock
Typesetter: Jouve India Pvt. Ltd.
Production controller: Lyndsey Rogers
Printed and bound by: Martins the Printers

Image credits: P14 (tl) Petr Toman/Shutterstock, (tm) Allstar Picture Library Ltd/Alamy,
(tr) Allstar Picture Library Ltd/Alamy, (bl) AF archive/Alamy, (br): Jeff Greenberg/Getty
Maps: © CollinsBartholomew

Acknowledgements
The publishers gratefully acknowledge the permission granted to reproduce the copyright material in this book. Every effort has been made to trace copyright holders and to obtain their permission for the use of copyright material. The publishers will gladly receive any information enabling them to rectify any error or omission at the first opportunity.

Contents

Question Key

Questions marked with a triangle test recall

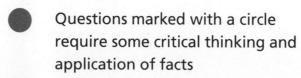

Questions marked with a circle require some critical thinking and application of facts

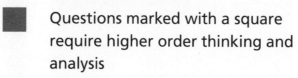

Questions marked with a square require higher order thinking and analysis

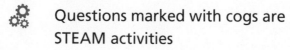

Questions marked with cogs are STEAM activities

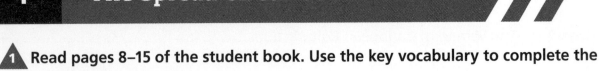

1 Read pages 8–15 of the student book. Use the key vocabulary to complete the crossword.

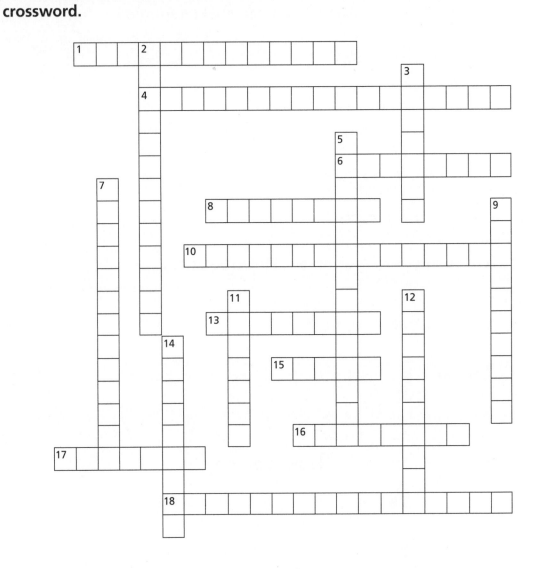

Across

1. Art or objects made by hand, e.g. pottery or weaving (4, 3, 6)

4. The spread of cultural beliefs and social activities from one community to another (8, 9)

6. The features of a culture, e.g. buildings, arts, traditions, from the past that are considered important

8. The traditional stories and beliefs of a cultural group

10. Places where something important happened in the past (10, 5)

13. A large group of people who have moved from their home country to another place

15. The type of clothes that are typical or traditional in a place or time

16. A person related to you who lived a long time ago, e.g. a great-grandparent

17. The beliefs, way of life and arts of a society, community or country

18. The shared culture, beliefs, language, etc. of a country which helps to make the people feel united (8, 8)

Down

2. A process that begins from when we are born by which we learn the values and traditions of culture

3. A style of cooking

5. A quality a person or thing has which makes them typical or noticeable

7. Consisting of or relating to people of several or many different cultures

9. A person who is related to you and who lives after you, e.g. a grandchild

11. Very different from each other

12. The process of leaving your country to live in another country

14. A person who comes to live in a country from another country

2 Read pages 12–15 of the student book, 'What is cultural diffusion?'. Are these sentences true or false?

a) Feng Shui is North American in origin. *True/False*

b) The acceptance of Feng Shui, Halloween and Thanksgiving into Jamaican life are all examples of cultural diffusion. *True/False*

c) Cultural diffusion has become less common in recent times. *True/False*

d) There are Caribbean festivals in Japan and Canada. *True/False*

e) The Notting Hill Carnival in London has become the largest jazz festival in Europe. *True/False*

f) People of a diaspora are usually quick to forget about the culture and heritage of their homeland. *True/False*

g) The African diaspora has spread across the Caribbean and American continents. It has been calculated that there are over 45 million people of the African diaspora living in the United States. *True/False*

h) The Jamaican diaspora stretches across and beyond the Caribbean. *True/False*

i) There is a large Jamaican community in Brixton, Birmingham. *True/False*

j) The main reason for Jamaican emigration has been to do with opportunities for employment. *True/False*

3 Rewrite the false sentences as true sentences.

_____

_____

_____

_____

_____

Complete the map of the Transatlantic Slave Trade routes.

a) Label the continents and ocean.

b) Shade the areas where Africans were captured.

c) Label the location of any **two** of the kingdoms from which Africans came.

d) Shade the areas where Africans were forced to settle.

e) Insert arrows to show the route of the enslaved people from Africa to the Americas and the Caribbean.

f) Insert labels to indicate the number of Africans settled in the Americas and the Caribbean.

g) Complete your map with a title and a key.

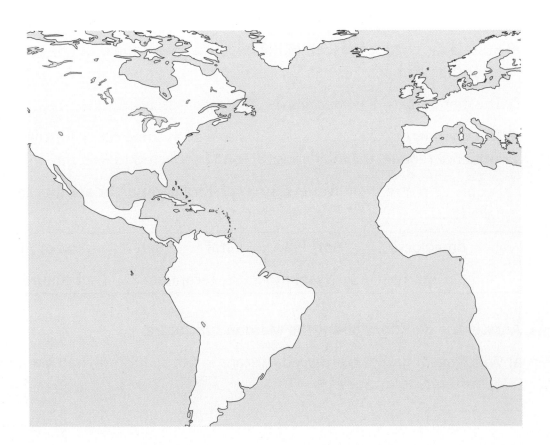

5 **Read pages 16–19 of the student book, 'Subcultures in Jamaica'. Complete the sentences about Rastafarian subculture using the word bank.**

a) Jamaica has a rich and diverse culture, including one main _____ of Rastafarianism.

b) Rastafarians see Haile Selassie as someone who can _____ them with their African origins.

c) Haile Selassie is represented by the _____, the King of Kings of Africa.

d) The Christian bible is important to Rastafarianism but their main religious text is the _____ and their god is called _____.

e) Rastafarians adopt the idea in the bible that hair should not be cut so they wear their hair in _____.

f) The diet of many Rastafarians is considered _____ .

g) The rhythms of _____, as well as some other African music, influence reggae, the main musical form connected to Rastafarianism.

h) People who give their lives in a struggle for liberation or another cause are called _____.

| dreadlocks | Holy Piby | Ital | Jah | Lion of Judah |
| martyrs | Nyabinghi | reconnect | subculture | |

6 **Answer the questions about the Maroon subculture.**

a) Which event gave the enslaved Africans in the Spanish-owned plantations the opportunity to escape?

_____

b) What happened in Accompong in the 17th century?

_____

c) What event does the Accompong Maroon Festival mark?

_____

7 Read pages 20–3 of the student book, 'How have different cultures influenced Jamaican culture'. Write the words and phrases of the positive influences and legacy for Jamaica in the correct box.

Taino	Spanish
_____	_____
_____	_____
_____	_____
_____	_____

British	African
_____	_____
_____	_____
_____	_____
_____	_____

bammy

domesticated animals   a judicial system

labour on plantations   a legal system   patwa

musical influences, e.g. Nyabinghi   name of the island of Jamaica

the official language of Jamaica   parliamentary government   plantation houses

rock carving and painting   sugar cane, bananas and citrus fruit

thatch roof housing   the first capital of Jamaica

the inspiration for Rastafarianism

8 Read pages 24–7 of the student book, 'How has globalisation affected Jamaican culture?'. Make notes about the ways globalisation has affected Jamaica in the correct sections of the diagram. You can add ideas from your research and ideas of your own.

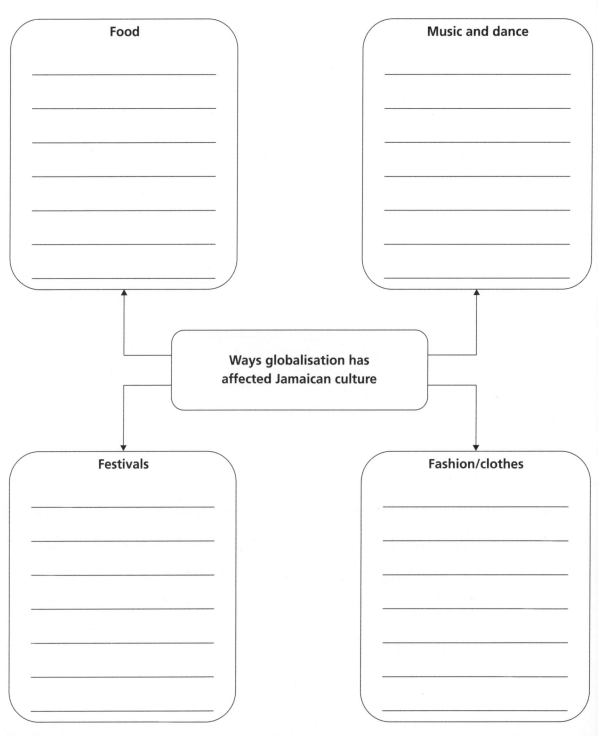

Food

Music and dance

Ways globalisation has affected Jamaican culture

Festivals

Fashion/clothes

9 Give examples of how Jamaica and the Jamaican diaspora have influenced other parts of the world under the following headings.

Food: _____

_____

_____

Music: _____

_____

_____

Festivals: _____

_____

_____

Religion: _____

_____

_____

Social and political movements: _____

_____

_____

10 Put these events and developments in the order they happened by numbering them from 1 to 8 to show the development of reggae music.

____Bob Marley becomes a Rastafarian

____death of Bob Marley

____early performances of Bob Marley and the Wailers

____mento

____rocksteady

____ska

____success of Bob Marley

____visit of Emperor Haile Selassie 1

11 Read pages 28–33 of the student book, 'How can we protect Jamaican culture in a globalised world?'. Identify the museum or public body from the descriptions.

a) It includes the Junior Centres which encourage young people to learn various art forms.

_____

b) It informs and encourages people to understand and respect the thoughts and writings of Marcus Garvey.

_____

c) It is home to the National Museum West and the National Gallery West.

_____

d) Its aim is to improve the awareness of the public of the contribution of African culture to Jamaica.

_____

e) Its aim is to maintain and develop cultural links between the Caribbean and Latin America.

_____

f) Its focus is on reggae and other forms of Jamaican music.

_____

g) This museum both collects plants and animals and educates the people on the need to value the wildlife of Jamaica.

_____

h) This museum collects and stores important documents about Jamaica and encourages research.

_____

i) This museum is the place to go if you want to learn about the history of Jamaican craft and technology.

_____

12 **Read pages 32–3 of the student book about cultural ambassadors.**

   a In your own words, explain what a cultural ambassador does.

      _____

      _____

   b Do some research to find out who has been recognised as a cultural ambassador.

      _____

      _____

   c Who else do you think could be recognised as a cultural ambassador?

      _____

13 **Research how Jamaican culture is promoted around the world.**

   a) Find the website of one Jamaican Embassy overseas and make notes on what they are doing to promote Jamaican culture.

      _____

      _____

      _____

      _____

   b) Watch the Jamaica Travel Channel and write a short description of one of the programmes that promotes Jamaican culture.

      _____

      _____

      _____

      _____

14 **Plan a video about one aspect of Jamaican culture that interests you.**

- Research your area of interest and, on a separate sheet of paper, make notes on what you want to include.
- Decide what you will feature in your video (e.g. interviews, photos, video clips).

15 Read pages 34–9 of the student book, 'How have creative industries and sport contributed to our national development?'. Use the photos to name the person who made each contribution to national development.

a) He was the first sportsperson to take 500 wickets in test cricket and was international cricketer of the year in 1987. _____

b) This artist developed a unique musical style fusing different elements to produce his own brand of reggae. _____

c) This artist worked tirelessly to promote Jamaican Patois and recognise it as an important part of the national heritage. _____

d) This artist's huge success around the world made him a symbol of Jamaican music and culture. _____

e) This sportsperson has won many international recognitions including World Athlete of the Year and World Sportsman of the year multiple times.

_____

f) This sportsperson represented Jamaica for 24 years and still holds world records in her events. _____

g) This artist wrote and performed poetry, songs and stories in Jamaican patois in many parts of the world. _____

h) This sportsperson represented the West Indies in 337 international matches over 17 years and was captain of the team for 22 matches. _____

i) This sportsperson won eight Olympic gold medals and was the most successful athlete of the World Championships. _____

j) This sportsperson won nine Olympic medals and 14 World Championship medals. _____

16 Research someone from the creative industries (music, literature, art and sculpture, drama, etc.) who has contributed to national identity. Make notes on the following aspects of their life and achievements.

Name:	
Life story	
Achievements	
Contribution to national identity	
Other points of interest	

1 **Read pages 46–7 of the student book, 'Regional integration' and complete the sentences.**

a) When countries in an area work together towards common goals, we call it _____.

b) Integration aims to give its members _____ in a group and to _____ and _____ that a group brings.

c) When people of different cultural backgrounds learn tolerance and respect for each other, we call it _____.

d) The definition of racial integration is _____ _____ so that they can live and work together.

e) Economic integration is when two or more states in a region set common economic goals and reduce _____.

f) A country's economy is made up of _____.

_____

g) The definition of cooperation is when people or countries _____

_____.

h) When you are dependent on other people, _____

_____

i) In order to strengthen their economies, from the 1950s onwards, some Caribbean states tried to _____.

j) When a number of countries sign a contract to work together or help each other, we call it a _____.

k) When two countries make an agreement to help each other, we call it a

_____.

l) Leaders of Caribbean states saw _____ as the way forward to help develop their countries.

Read pages 48–51 of the student book. Complete the timeline with the seven events in the box.

> A referendum on membership of the WIF held in Jamaica   Belize joins CARIFTA
>
> CARIFTA formed   Meeting held to discuss a free trade region
>
> More countries join CARIFTA   West Indian Federation disbanded
>
> West Indian Federation formed

1958_____

1959_____

1960_____

1961_____

1962_____

1963_____

1964_____

1965_____

1966_____

1967_____

1968_____

1969_____

1970_____

1971_____

3 **Answer the questions about the West Indian Federation.**

a) What was the primary intention of the West Indian Federation?

_____

b) Select any two of the factors that caused the West Indian Federation to be disbanded and explain why they contributed to the failure of the organisation.

_____

_____

4 **Read pages 50–55 of the student book. Then read the statements below and write CARIFTA, CARICOM, CSME or OECS next to each one.**

a) It was formed to promote unity and solidarity amongst its members, which were mainly the territories of the Lesser Antilles. _____

b) One economic objective is expansion of trade and economic relations, which already existed among the members of CARICOM. _____

c) It promotes cooperation and integration between member states, especially in areas like trade and transportation. _____

d) The member states bought and sold more goods amongst themselves under this first free trade agreement. _____

e) Trade between member states was liberalised with the signing of this agreement at Dickenson Bay. _____

f) It allows free movement of money and skilled labour between member states, which did not exist before in any of the other agreements.

_____

g) It allows people to move around freely to study and to look for work.

_____

h) Anguilla, the British Virgin Islands and Montserrat are associate members.

_____

i) It enables states to respond as a group to the challenges or opportunities of globalisation. _____

j) It tried to make sure that there was fair competition, especially for smaller businesses. _____

k) This organisation coordinates foreign policy for its members. _____

l) This is an inter-governmental organisation formed in 1981. _____

m) It came into being with the signing of the Treaty of Chaguaramas in 1973.

_____

n) One of its key objectives is to expand and deepen the level of regional integration among its members and at the same time improve on the work carried out under a previous agreement. _____

5 Read the scenarios below and explain why each one is considered beneficial to both citizens and also the member states of the different organisations.

	Benefit to the individual	Benefit to the country
I am a business man in Jamaica and when CARIFTA was formed and the countries agreed to no quota on goods I was very happy. My business started to boom after this and as my business grew, my community also benefitted.		
My father has just opened up another branch of his business in Trinidad and one in Grenada and it was very easy for him to do so. I noticed that there are also some Trinidadian companies here in Jamaica. All of this is because of the agreement under the CSME that allows persons to set up businesses in any CARICOM country. It has been good for both Jamaica and Trinidad.		
'Rosie, I heard that your son has just finished his training as a carpenter. You should encourage him to go and apply for the CARICOM Skills Certificate because the new CSME agreement allows free movement of labour. It allows him to work freely in any CARICOM country. That's what my daughter, who is a nurse, did and she's working now in St Lucia.'		

6 Read pages 58–63 of the student book. Then use the word bank to complete each section below.

Medicine

_____

_____

Culture

_____

_____

Sport

_____

_____

Education

_____

_____

CARIFESTA	occupational health
Caribbean Examination Council	environmental management
cultural bonds	international tournaments
research facilities	CARIFTA games

7 Draw lines to match the words or phrases to their meanings.

a) unity

i) A situation in which people, groups or countries work together to achieve a result that will benefit them all.

b) integrated

ii) The characteristics that make a person, place or event different from others.

c) cooperation

iii) A situation in which people, societies or countries are linked by their cultures and values.

d) identity

iv) Joined together into one group, unit or system.

e) cultural bond

v) A situation in which people, communities or countries are joined together or agree about something.

8 Read pages 64–5 of the student book, 'The Caribbean Court of Justice'. Then find the words in the puzzle below. The words can be vertical or horizontal. There are 9 words to find.

```
T  A  C  C  E  S  S  I  B  I  L  I  T  Y
R  F  H  I  G  V  I  N  X  J  N  N  U  G
A  P  G  W  S  T  X  X  L  B  F  R  H  I
N  J  U  D  I  C  I  A  L  Y  B  R  J  A
S  Q  F  A  F  P  U  F  T  O  R  I  O  M
P  I  N  T  E  G  R  I  T  Y  E  O  T  U
A  Q  B  Y  F  Y  Q  Q  X  T  A  C  Z  N
R  O  Q  L  J  D  A  I  Q  E  C  E  G  I
E  N  A  X  J  A  C  W  P  M  H  D  U  C
N  J  U  R  I  S  D  I  C  T  I  O  N  I
C  O  U  R  T  E  S  Y  C  U  S  G  U  P
Y  P  K  E  P  H  W  J  F  C  W  Y  C  A
H  Y  B  R  I  D  L  Y  C  J  R  D  J  L
```

9 Match the definitions with words from the puzzle above.

a) The quality of being easy to obtain or use _____

b) To break or fail to observe a law _____

c) Showing politeness, respect and care for others _____

d) A mixture of two different systems or things _____

e) The quality of being honest and doing the right thing _____

f) Relating to the legal system and administration of justice _____

g) The area or state in which a court has authority _____

h) Relating to a town or city that has its own local government

_____

i) The quality of being easily understood or recognised _____

21

10 Read pages 66–7 of the student book, 'Regional integration and cooperation'. Explain briefly how regional integration can help, or might have helped, in each of the scenarios below.

A. The Statistical Institute of Jamaica reported recently that unemployment in Jamaica has continued to decrease. This has been the trend since 2013 but it warned that, despite the decrease, unemployment in Jamaica is very high.

_____

_____

_____

_____

B. When I go to the supermarket, I see a wide range of products that will allow me to 'pick, choose and refuse' but what I like even more is to see that the products are from other Caribbean countries.

_____

_____

_____

_____

C. 'Did you notice how many Caribbean countries stepped in to help the people of St Vincent and Grenadines recently when the volcano erupted? It was such a good thing to see the different agencies working to ensure people were safe and reduce the amount of damage the country experienced.'

_____

_____

_____

_____

Complete the crossword. All the words are from 2.5–2.11 of the student book.

Across

2. A particular place or group of people that a product is sold to

4. Something that happens in nature and causes damage or kills many people (7, 8)

5. The qualities that make someone or something what they are and different from other people

11. Capable of continuing having visitors for a long time at the same level (11, 7)

13. The careful use of something so that it is not lost or destroyed

14. Money or property that can be used to start or invest in a business

15. Items that someone owns that can be moved from one place to another

16. Combining things, people or ideas into one effective unit, group or system

17. Conditions and processes relating to people's health, especially the systems that supply water and deal with human waste

18. Freedom from control by another country

19. The workers in a country, industry or company

Down

1. A government department

3. Something that gives people a reason to love one another or feel they have a duty to each other because of what they have in common (8, 5)

6. A situation in which people, groups or countries join together or agree about something

7. A celebration showing the similarities and differences among different groups of people (8, 8)

8. Able to attend certain meetings (8, 6)

9. A group of people or a country that is not allowed to take part in all of another group's activities (9, 6)

10. To make a situation or state continue without changing

12. An arrangement between two or more countries on trade between them (5, 9)

16. Involving governments of different countries (5-12)

12 Read pages 68–73 of the student book. Then join the beginnings of the sentences in Column A with the correct ending in Column B. Record your answers below.

a) _____   b) _____   c) _____   d) _____

e) _____   f) _____   g) _____   h) _____

i) _____   j) _____   k) _____   l) _____

Column A	Column B
a) Regional integration has given businesses and industries in the Caribbean	i) access to a larger market.
b) Trade expansion means a diversification of products	ii) the costs of production and offers economies of scale.
c) Regional integration also creates jobs,	iii) which means people have more money.
d) Working cooperatively to produce certain goods reduces	iv) available to larger markets.
e) CARICOM is a highly trade-dependent region undergoing	v) and greater collaboration is crucial to tackle common challenges.
f) To realise the CSME vision, the member countries must focus energies	vi) major changes to its economic relationships with the world.
g) Differing export and production structures and income levels mean it can be challenging	vii) on much deeper commitments to integration.
h) The Caribbean authorities generally agree that integration should remain a top priority	viii) to integrate economic and structural policies.
i) Businesses often need investment to	ix) based in different countries in the region, and often produce a number of different products.
j) The role of government includes making sure that	x) expand or bring in new equipment.
k) The role of businesses in regional integration includes	xi) increasing the range of goods and services.
l) Multinational companies are large companies that are	xii) legislation works across the region.

1 Read pages 80–3 of the student book. Write the word or words that mean the following.

a) An issue within a community that affects a number of people which the community wants correcting   a _____ _____

b) Solved or putting right   _____

c) Not the usual or accepted standards or ways of behaving   _____

d) Serious criminal activities that are planned and controlled by powerful groups _____ _____

e) Complicated and difficult   _____

f) An action or activity that is an offence and can be punished by law _____

g) Not having things that people consider essential in life, e.g. a home, education _____

h) Feeling or showing a sense that things are so bad that you can do nothing about it   _____

i) A change or development in a situation to become lower or less _____ _____

j) The importance or respect that a person has among a group _____

k) Related to physical possessions (e.g. clothes, jewellery, cars) or money rather than ideas or values   _____

l) Not operating normally or properly, often used to describe relationships that are not working as they should   _____

m) The influence from other members of a social group to act in the same way as them   _____

n) Frightened and lacking in confidence to deal with the situation a person is in _____

2 Read pages 84–5 of the student book, 'Sexual health'. Answer the questions.

a) How are chlamydia and gonorrhoea treated? _____

b) How is Hepatitis B carried? _____

c) What is the good news about syphilis? _____

d) Why should pregnant women be tested for STIs? _____

e) What is the HIV rate in Jamaica? _____

3 Make short notes on how each of the following factors cause HIV/AIDS infection to be higher among vulnerable groups. You can do further research to help with your answers.

Poverty	
Gender	
Discrimination	

4 Write a letter to the editor of a local newspaper arguing for cheaper medications and counselling services for persons with HIV/AIDS. Explain why this is important in helping to reduce the spread of the virus.

_____

_____

_____

_____

_____

_____

_____

_____

5 Read pages 86–7 of the student book, 'Teenage pregnancy'. Complete the sentences below on causes of teenage pregnancy and actions that can be taken.

Some of the causes of teenage pregnancy are:

a) _____ and myths about contraception.

b) _____ _____ _____ free contraception.

c) _____ (high-risk sexual activity, poor contraceptive use, involvement in crime, etc.).

d) _____ factors (low achievement, lack of interest in school, leaving school early).

e) _____ background factors (poverty, being a child of teenage parents, being in care, etc.).

f) _____ factors (where the young person lives, unemployment rate).

Some possible actions to tackle teenage pregnancy are:

g) _____ _____ to young people about sex and relationships.

h) Ensuring that young people understand information about them is

_____

i) Providing contraceptive _____ _____ _____ about pregnancy and abortion.

j) _____ _____ of contraception.

k) _____ _____ that schools provide contraceptive services.

l) Offering a _____ _____ _____ for teenage mothers.

6 Select one of the causes above and write a short paragraph on how this factor contributes to teenage pregnancy. Use a separate sheet of paper.

7 Read pages 88–91 of the student book. Then complete the sentences using the scrambled words.

a) The definition of child abuse is when a child is _____ harmed by an adult or another child. [nlaenyilotitn]

b) _____ of a child is when he or she is not given love, care or attention. [gcetnle]

c) Various _____ have been developed by the government as a response to child abuse. [stegitrase]

d) Part of the action plan has been to _____ the policy to protect children. [snhrttgene]

e) Public education about violence prevention, the care of child victims and children's rights have been _____. [neendhac]

f) The NPACV is _____ and evaluated to make sure its work is effective. [ortedimno]

g) There are numerous forms of domestic abuse, including _____ abuse when someone deliberately hurts or injures another person. [pyishalc]

h) _____ abuse is when someone seriously upsets or causes distress to another person. [tnaomeloi]

i) Other types of domestic abuse are sexual and _____. [iciflaann]

j) When a woman or girl is murdered, it is called _____. [iemfiedc]

k) The traditional view that men are superior to women and that they have the right to control their women is called a _____ attitude or view. [aaihtclprar]

l) A majority of Jamaicans believe that the man is the head of the household and women's duties are raising children and _____ duties. [cdsoimte]

m) One reason for men abusing or killing their partners is when they feel inferior to their partner, when they have anger problems or they feel a lot of. _____. [olajusye]

n) Now that more and more women are working they have become less _____ on their husbands financially. [edepenntd]

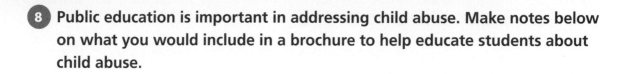

8 Public education is important in addressing child abuse. Make notes below on what you would include in a brochure to help educate students about child abuse.

Forms of child abuse	
Signs of child abuse	
Preventing child abuse	
Agencies responsible for children welfare	

9 Examine the factors that contribute to domestic violence. Explain how any three of these factors may also cause a child to be abused at home.

_____

_____

_____

_____

_____

_____

_____

_____

_____

10 Using the diagram on page 91 and your own research, explain why the Covid-19 pandemic has caused an increase in domestic violence. Use a separate sheet of paper.

11 **Follow these steps to research a social issue in your community or school.**

a) Select one of the social issues featured in the student book.

b) Design a research topic on the issue. This should be written in the form of a question (e.g. *What are the main factors influencing domestic abuse in my community? What are the main effects of juvenile delinquency on families in my community?*). Make sure your teacher approves your topic before conducting the research.

_____

c) You can gather the data you need for the research by using a questionnaire. Create a list of five questions you will use for your questionnaire. Make sure your questions will not offend anyone and will not ask about personal and private information. Show these to your teacher to ensure they are suitable. After your teacher approves the questions, ask 10 persons in your community to answer the questions.

_____

_____

_____

_____

_____

d) After collecting your data, write a brief report on your findings. Remember to use statistical data in your description (e.g. 20% believes the main cause of domestic violence is…).

_____

_____

_____

_____

_____

e) Write a brief conclusion for your research. Your conclusion helps to answer your research question.

_____

_____

1 Read pages 104–7 of the student book. Draw lines to match the terms to their meanings.

a) sustainable development	**i)** A group of people with something in common, e.g. their age.
b) finite natural resources	**ii)** A process that leads to growth and positive change without using all the resources, so that future generations can also use them.
c) urban development	**iii)** A type of graph that shows the age and sex of the population.
d) rural development	**iv)** Growth and progress made in areas outside of towns and cities.
e) demography	**v)** Growth and progress made in towns and cities.
f) life expectancy	**vi)** How long people are expected to live.
g) dependents	**vii)** People who are supported by others because they are too young, old or ill to work.
h) population pyramid	**viii)** The kind of things that cannot be replaced once they have been used (e.g. oil, gold).
i) cohort	**ix)** The study of population.

2 Make notes on the advantages and disadvantages of living in rural and urban areas. Use what you talked about in the Discussion on page 105 of the student book.

	Rural	Urban
Advantages		
Disadvantages		

3 Mark and label the towns in the major urban areas. Use page 106 of the student book and your atlas to complete this task.

4 Use your phone or tablet to find a recent population pyramid for the world. Compare it to the 2017 population pyramid of Jamaica on page 107 of the student book.

a) For what year is your world population pyramid? _____

b) What was the total world population when the pyramid was made?

_____

c) Which was the largest cohort? _____

d) Which is the largest cohort for the 2017 pyramid for Jamaica?

_____

e) Why do you think there is this difference? _____

_____

f) In the oldest age groups of the Jamaica 2017 pyramid, what do you notice about the number of males and females? _____

g) Is this the same for the world population? _____

h) Why do you think this is? _____

_____

5 Read pages 108–111 of the student book. Complete the sentences by selecting the correct term from the word bank.

a) The _____ _____ are the people who are of working age and able to work.

b) An increase in the amount of goods and services produced per head of population is called _____ _____.

c) The customs, traditions, values and beliefs of a country are the _____ _____ that can help to grow an economy.

d) The value of Jamaica's goods and services produced in a year is known as its annual _____ _____ _____.

e) The Jamaican _____ _____ _____ includes the economic activities of people and businesses in other countries.

f) The policies and programmes a government chooses are _____ _____ that have an effect on the growth of an economy.

g) The skills, knowledge and experience of the workers in a country is referred to as the _____ _____ of the country.

h) Tools and machinery that enable workers to produce more goods are examples of _____ _____ _____.

i) When there is _____ _____ the new technology allows workers to produce more goods, often more quickly and cheaply.

economic growth	physical capital goods	technological improvement
labour force	human capital	gross domestic product
gross national product	social factors	political factors

6 Complete the following sentences about the Human Development Index (HDI).

The HDI is used to follow a) _____ _____ _____ over time and to b) _____ the levels of different countries. The HDI is measured using c) the average number of years of _____, d) the _____ _____ at birth, e) the _____ _____ _____ per person.

Are these sentence true or false?

a) An increase in the amount of goods and services produced over a period of time is known as development. *True/False*

b) A healthy population and a large labour force serves to encourage economic growth. *True/False*

c) GDP measures what the people living in a country earn in a year. *True/False*

d) Higher living standards for the people lead to sustained economic growth. *True/False*

e) A growing economy leads to more taxes collected by the government. *True/False*

f) The quantity of the human resources available to an economy refers to the skills, training, education, etc. of the workforce. *True/False*

g) Oil, natural gas and minerals are examples of natural resources. *True/False*

h) Land, building and machinery are examples of capital goods. *True/False*

i) Jamaica's HDI position in 2017 showed it was approximately in the middle of the range of countries measured. *True/False*

j) The HDI measures job satisfaction, job security and level of freedom in a country. *True/False*

8 **Rewrite the false sentences as true sentences.**

_____

_____

_____

_____

_____

_____

_____

_____

_____

9 Read pages 112–15 of the student book. Then complete the sentences using words and phrases from the word bank. (Note that not all of the words/phrases are used.)

a) _____ are amenities that the citizens of a country need, such as transport, health care and power supply.

b) The material things that are made to be sold are called _____.

c) The type of resources that are made by people and we can see and touch, e.g. buildings, machinery and other equipment are known as _____ _____.

d) We use the term _____ _____ to describe people and the skills and abilities that they have.

e) _____ is the information and understanding which people have.

f) Your _____ are your knowledge and ability that enable you to do something well.

g) We call your natural ability to do something well _____.

h) _____ _____ describes resources that have been made or found and that we can use to produce goods or services.

i) We often talk about _____ and _____ together: the first refers to how good or bad something is, the second concerns how many or how much there is.

j) When we talk about the make-up of a population, such as their age, gender, religion, or ethnicity, we call it the _____ of the population.

k) In many countries it is illegal to discriminate people on the basis of their race or _____.

l) We all know that _____ is required to be an artist, musician or writer but it is equally important when coming up with new ideas in many areas of life.

ability	composition	creativity	economy	gender
goods	human resources	knowledge	physical capital	physical resources
quality	quantity	services	skills	talent

10 Two words from the word bank in activity 9 have not been used. Write sentences of your own using these words.

_____

_____

_____

_____

11 Look at the pie charts on page 114 of the student book.

a) What was the second most common ethnic origin in Jamaica in 2011?

_____

b) What was the main religion in Jamaica in 2011? _____

c) Why do you think pie charts are useful for representing this kind of information?

_____

d) Use your phone, tablet or a computer to do some research on the age of the labour force in Jamaica in 2019. Find out how many workers there were in different age groups. Then create a pie chart like the ones on page 114 of the student book to represent the information.

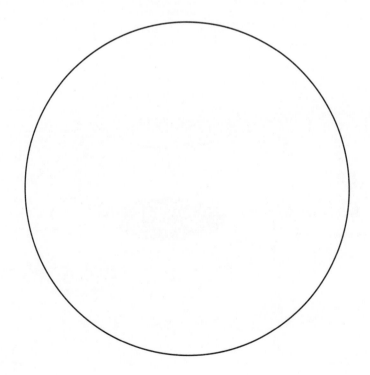

12 Read pages 116–19 of the student book. Then look at the list of what skilled, educated people can offer on page 116. Choose three factors and explain how each factor can benefit the economy.

1. _____

_____

_____

2. _____

_____

_____

3. _____

_____

_____

13 Complete the examples in the mind map. Then add at least one more example of your own for each section.

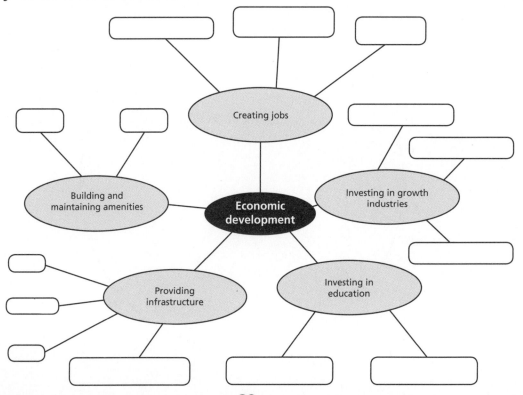

14 Explain how two of the following help to contribute to economic development in a country: a) creating jobs, b) providing infrastructure, c) investing in education.

i) _____

_____

_____

ii) _____

_____

_____

15 For each statement, choose the best answer, i, ii or iii.

a) The overall aim of economic development is to improve:

i) a country's standard of living.

ii) the standard of education.

iii) the number of skilled, educated people.

b) Attitudes to education in Jamaica changed:

i) before 1950.

ii) during the 1950s and 1960s.

iii) in recent years.

c) Nowadays, education is seen as:

i) a burden on the state.

ii) a way to teach social values, customs and religion.

iii) an investment in the future.

d) Human resource development (HRD) aims to:

i) send students to colleges and universities.

ii) develop a highly-skilled workforce.

iii) help people earn more money.

16 Read pages 120–1 of the student book, 'Our physical resources'.
Complete the diagrams to summarise the information.

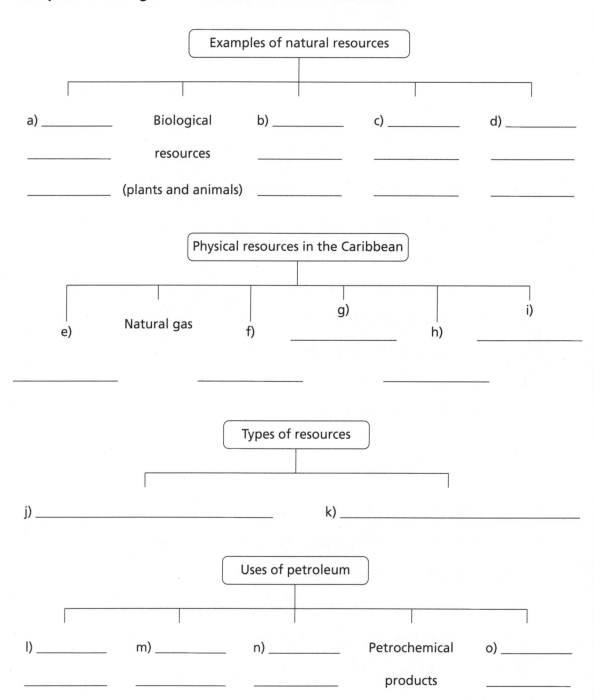

Examples of natural resources

a) _____   Biological   b) _____   c) _____   d) _____

_____   resources   _____   _____   _____

_____   (plants and animals)   _____   _____   _____

Physical resources in the Caribbean

e)   Natural gas   f)   g)   h)   i)

_____   _____   _____   _____

Types of resources

j) _____   k) _____

Uses of petroleum

l) _____   m) _____   n) _____   Petrochemical   o) _____

_____   _____   _____   products   _____

17 Find the names of twelve physical resources from other Caribbean countries in the puzzle below. The words can be vertical, horizontal or diagonal. Write the names of the resources with the country/countries where they are found.

```
U  N  E  K  U  X  Y  J  H  Y  I  E  O  G  L  H
B  P  V  B  Z  K  K  T  E  E  Z  E  I  O  M  I
X  H  P  Z  R  A  K  I  E  N  Y  F  Z  L  T  P
B  Y  A  D  O  Q  A  M  P  R  P  L  O  D  Y  C
A  D  H  F  I  S  H  B  U  F  R  B  N  U  D  T
U  R  I  E  R  O  U  E  M  T  M  F  D  L  Z  C
X  O  B  Z  N  J  F  R  I  E  Q  Y  W  Q  J  C
I  P  P  T  R  O  P  I  C  A  L  F  R  U  I  T
T  O  S  U  G  N  T  U  E  I  O  N  Z  S  A  H
E  W  S  R  L  A  I  A  Y  G  C  Q  F  L  V  F
R  E  A  D  I  A  M  O  N  D  S  E  R  U  L  Z
R  R  L  N  A  T  U  R  A  L  G  A  S  P  E  C
C  G  T  B  Q  R  U  O  Z  H  A  V  V  D  G  M
P  E  T  R  O  L  E  U  M  B  Z  X  D  O  P  S
A  R  A  B  L  E  L  A  N  D  X  F  N  Z  V  P
```

Resource   Country/countries

_____   _____

_____   _____

_____   _____

_____   _____

_____   _____

_____   _____

_____   _____

_____   _____

_____   _____

_____   _____

_____   _____

_____   _____

18 Read pages 122–5 of the student book. Label the map to show the location of alumina plants (A), cement works (C), oil refineries (O) and gypsum mines (G). Shade the bauxite mining areas.

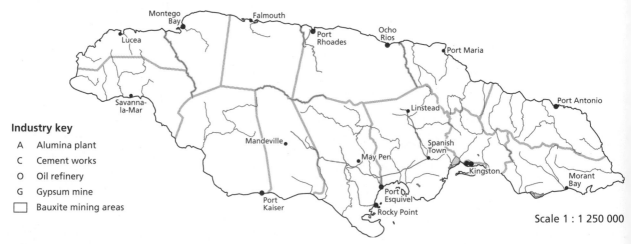

Industry key

A Alumina plant
C Cement works
O Oil refinery
G Gypsum mine
☐ Bauxite mining areas

Scale 1 : 1 250 000

19 Label the map to show the location of oil fields (O), gas fields (G), bauxite (B), gold (Gd) and nickel (N).

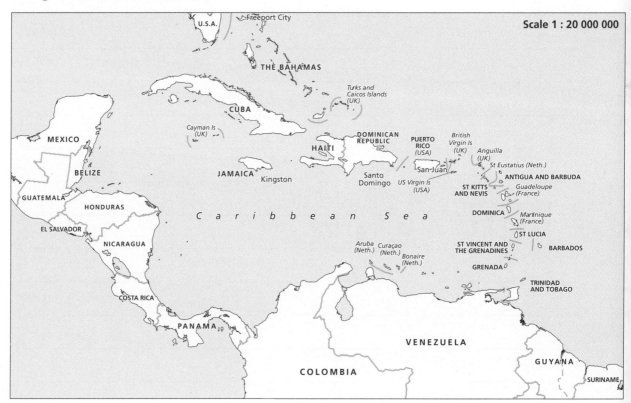

Scale 1 : 20 000 000

Energy and minerals key

O Oil fields   G Gas fields   B Bauxite   Gd Gold   N Nickel

20 Read pages 126–9 of the student book. Match the words with their meanings.

a)	maximise	**i)**	Causing little or no damage to the environment so can be continued for many years. _____
b)	yield	**ii)**	Covering the soil with something to keep in moisture. _____
c)	monocropping	**iii)**	Growing a single crop year after year on the same land. _____
d)	soil erosion	**iv)**	The amount of something that is produced. _____
e)	deforestation	**v)**	The permanent removal of trees to make room for something else rather than forest. _____
f)	sustainable	**vi)**	The washing or blowing away of the top layer of the soil making the soil poorer. _____
g)	replenish	**vii)**	To fill something up again. _____
h)	mulching	**viii)**	The long-term heating of the Earth's climate._____
i)	exploitation	**ix)**	The action of using and benefitting resources, maybe over-using and making the resource unavailable for the future. _____
j)	global warming	**x)**	To get the most out of something. _____

21 Make notes to compare the advantages and disadvantages of conventional, large-scale farming.

Advantages	Disadvantages
_____	_____
_____	_____
_____	_____
_____	_____
_____	_____
_____	_____

22 **Use a computer, a tablet or your phone to research agriculture in Jamaica.**

a) Find out which crops are planted in Jamaica and where they are grown. Indicate which ones are grown on a large scale. Compile your information in a table in the space below.

b) Find out how many people are currently employed in the agriculture sector. Compare the numbers for three years and briefly describe any change.

_____

_____

_____

_____

c) Find out how much money Jamaica earns from agriculture. Compare with one other sector (e.g. tourism) and comment on any differences seen.

_____

_____

_____

_____

23 **Complete the diagram about the uses of water.**

   i) Add the examples from the text on page 128 of the student book

   ii) Add other examples of your own.

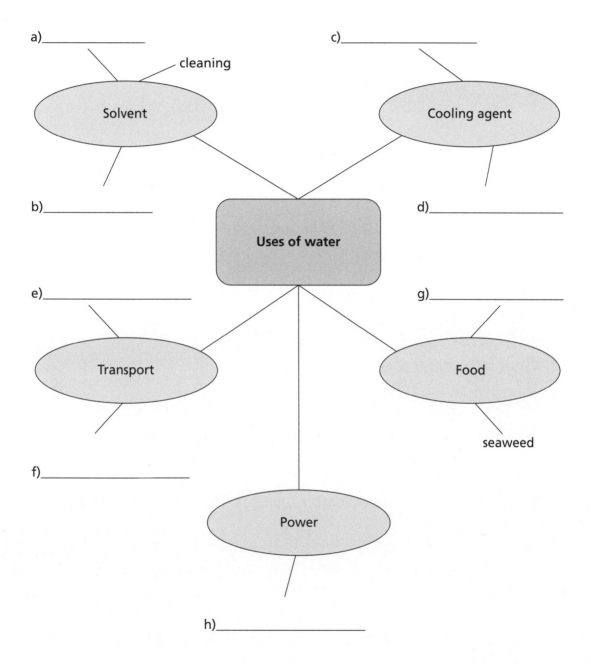

a)_____

cleaning

Solvent

b)_____

c)_____

Cooling agent

d)_____

Uses of water

e)_____

Transport

f)_____

g)_____

Food

seaweed

Power

h)_____

24 Read pages 130–7 of the student book. Then answer the questions.

a) What is an economic recession?

_____

b) What are the usual results of a recession?

_____

c) How do natural disasters affect economic development?

_____

d) Which risks have increased for Jamaica as a result of climate change?

_____

e) What is Jamaica's vision statement?

_____

f) What is the Vision 2030 plan aiming to encourage?

_____

g) What is the difference between Vision 2030 and earlier plans?

_____

h) Which of the four goals of Vision 2030 has seen the most progress?

_____

i) Which of the four goals of Vision 2030 has seen the least progress?

_____

j) What have been the greatest gains under *Goal 3: Jamaica's economy is prosperous*?

_____

k) Under which goal does hurricane preparedness come?

_____

25 **Use a computer, tablet or phone to research the achievements of Vision 2030.**

The table below shows some of the areas in which Jamaica made either significant progress or has surpassed the Vision 2030 targets in 2016/17. Conduct research online to find out what the levels for these areas were in 2016/17 and what they were like 3–5 years before.

	2016/17 figures	3–5 years before figures
Lower inflation rates		
Increased tourism (tourist arrivals in the island)		
Life expectancy		
Child mortality rate		
Grade 4 literacy rate		
Grade 4 numeracy rate		
Secondary school enrolment rate		

26 **Now write a brief analysis of what you discovered from the research.**

_____

_____

_____

_____

_____

_____

_____

_____

_____

_____

_____

1 **Read pages 144–9 of the student book. Then unscramble the words to give the word being defined.**

a) The group of people who are responsible for managing a country. [tevongnrme] _____

b) A system of government in which citizens have a say in the decisions that affect their lives. [emcdcyaor] _____

c) Someone who legally belongs to a country is a [ictiezn] of that country. _____

d) You are [liegielb] to do something if you are qualified or able to do it. _____

e) A set of laws by which a country is governed. [oiustctonnti] _____

f) When a country or smaller state separates from a larger group. [soeiencss] _____

g) If law and order breaks down as a result of the absence of a government, we call it [arnaych]. _____

h) A [tritenseperaev] democracy is one in which the people elect officials to govern for them. _____

i) Being careful to say and do things which will not offend or anger other people. [mplictaoid] _____

j) The act of taking part in something. [ciaropntiipta] _____

k) A vote on a matter of public importance. [ederumerfn] _____

l) To succeed in doing something. [pcamsioclh] _____

2 **Explain the terms in your own words.**

a) Majority rule _____

_____

b) Minority rights _____

_____

3 **Find answers to the questions and do some research.**

a) Name an example from the student book of a situation in which a referendum was used.

_____

_____

b) In the referendum, 54.1% voted 'no'. What percentage voted 'yes'? _____

c) 61.5% of eligible voters actually voted. In your opinion, is that percentage high enough to be accepted? Do you think voters should always vote in an election or referendum? Justify your opinion in a few sentences.

_____

_____

_____

_____

d) Give an example of secession from your student book. _____

_____

_____

e) Find another example of secession. _____

_____

f) What happened? _____

_____

_____

g) Find an example of a country falling into anarchy. _____

_____

h) What happened? _____

_____

_____

4 Read pages 150–5 of the student book, 'Structure of central government'. Complete the summaries of the three branches of Jamaican government.

Role of the legislature

a) makes _____

b) approves _____

c) amends _____

d) monitors _____

e) The **executive** is made up of members of the **cabinet**. The cabinet:

   i)   controls _____

   ii) is responsible for _____

   iii) consists of _____

   iv) ministers are responsible for _____

f) The **judiciary** oversees justice. The courts of Jamaica are:

   i)   _____

   ii) _____

   iii) _____

5 Conduct research about the three branches of government in Jamaica.

   a) Explain the main difference between the House of Representatives and the Senate.

   _____

   _____

b) Describe the current make-up of the House of Representatives and Senate. Include how many people are from the ruling party and opposition, and the names of the President of the Senate and Speaker of the House.

_____

_____

_____

_____

c) Name the current ministries and the names of the ministers for each.

_____

_____

_____

_____

_____

_____

d) Find out about different court cases and, on a separate sheet of paper, write a brief description of each and their outcomes.

   i) A case in which the person was found to be innocent and relieved of all charges.

   _____

   ii) A case in which the person was found guilty and sentenced to serve a period in prison.

   _____

6 **Look at 'How a Bill Becomes Law' on page 152 of the student book.**

You are a member of the House of Representatives in Jamaica. You put forward a bill to the House on the use of drones in public spaces. Write a description of the process the bill went through, any obstacles it faced and the outcome at the end. Use a separate sheet of paper.

7 Read pages 156–9 of the student book. Complete the notes on the responsibilities of local government using the word bank.

Some responsibilities of local government are:

a) _____, b) _____ and c) _____ roads and public facilities

d) _____ that local services function

e) _____ building and planning approvals, and also

f) _____ trades and businesses

g) _____ non-governmental organisations and other agencies

h) _____ national policies and development programmes

i) _____ plans and initiatives for the development of the parish, and for

j) _____ economic activity and wealth creation

boosting	coordinating	developing	ensuring	implementing
licensing	maintaining	managing	regulating	supporting

8 Write the name of the agency (ODPEM, SDC or NSWMA) which has responsibility for the following:

a) Advancing sport _____

b) Coordinating emergency response to disaster events _____

c) Cultural and economic development _____

d) Pest or nuisance control _____

e) Encouraging good governance and economic prosperity _____

f) Identifying disaster threats _____

g) Setting up waste disposal sites _____

h) Organising relief operations _____

9   Draw lines to join the beginnings of the sentences in Column A with the correct ending in Column B to describe the functions of central and local government.

Column A		Column B
CENTRAL GOVERNMENT		
a) Raise revenue		i) by providing police and armed forces for internal and external protection.
b) Maintain law and order		ii) such as roads, water, power, sewage, etc.
c) Develop economic policies		iii) to avoid conflicts and develop trade and finance.
d) Run social services		iv) to encourage business and create employment.
e) Ensure national security		v) to protect citizens.
f) Build relationships with other countries		vi) to provide for the health, education, etc. of the people.
g) Build and maintain national infrastructure		vii) to spend on social services.
LOCAL GOVERNMENT		
h) Construct and maintain local infrastructure		viii) such as drainage and maintenance of rivers.
i) Provide and maintain community services		ix) such as local transport, markets, libraries, recreation and childcare facilities and homes for elderly people.
j) Collecting and disposing of rubbish		x) such as minor roads, bridges, road signs and pedestrian crossings.
k) Providing land development services		xi) to maintain public health and the environment.

1   Complete the crossword with words from pages 166–9 of the student book.

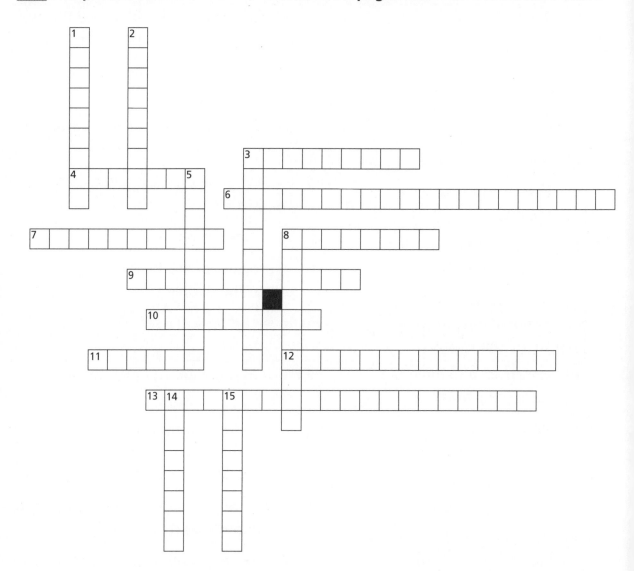

Across

3. A person who seeks to be nominated or elected to a position in the national or local government

4. A person who has the right to vote in an election

6. One of the people competing in an election who is not a member of one of the main political parties (11, 9)

7. People who believe in the ideas of a particular person or group

8. An event at which people choose a person who will serve them in local and national government

9. An area of a country that elects a representative to parliament

10. A statement that publicly states what a candidate's views are on certain issues and explains the policies they support or will introduce if they are elected

11. People supporting their choice of a person or an issue in an election

12. A politician who is a member of the government

13. A system whereby people vote for candidates who, if they get enough votes and are elected, serve in the government (10, 10)

Down

1. Officially suggested that someone should stand for parliament

2. A system of government in which people vote in elections to choose the people who will govern them

3. A person who lives in an area and can vote for who they want to represent them in local and national elections

5. An elected politician _____ his or her constituents

8. All the people in a country who are eligible and registered to vote in an election

14. Legally allowed or qualified to do something

15. A series of events that are organised to help a candidate get elected

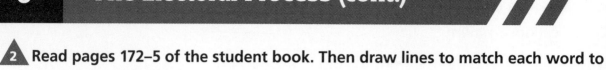

2 Read pages 172–5 of the student book. Then draw lines to match each word to the correct definition.

a)	ballot paper	**i)**	The right that people have to vote in elections.
b)	nomination	**ii)**	To have the right to vote.
c)	franchise	**iii)**	Something on which someone records their vote next to the name of a candidate.
d)	ballot box	**iv)**	The day when people register to stand as a candidate.
e)	adult suffrage	**v)**	This allows people to vote anonymously and freely.
f)	secret ballot	**vi)**	A special container which is sealed so that people cannot tamper with it.
g)	Nomination Day	**vii)**	A vote or a piece of paper on which a person records their vote.
h)	ballot	**viii)**	The procedure candidates have to follow in order to stand for election.

3 Read the case study on page 173 of the student book. Then number the following procedures from 1 to 6 in the order they take place on Nomination Day in Jamaica.

a) The candidates' deposits are taken to the treasury. _____

b) The candidates' information is sent to the Electoral Office. _____

c) Each candidate makes a statutory declaration that they are properly qualified to be nominated as a candidate. _____

d) The ballot papers are printed. _____

e) Candidates present themselves to returning officers in their respective constituencies with six electors from their constituencies in order to be nominated. _____

f) Each candidate makes a deposit of $3000 for their nomination. _____

4 Join the beginnings of the sentences in Column A with the correct ending in Column B.

a _____   g _____

b _____   h _____

c _____   i _____

d _____   j _____

e _____   k _____

f _____   l _____

Column A	Column B
a) People who are enfranchised	i) all adult citizens are enfranchised.
b) Until the 1920s suffrage	ii) have the right to vote.
c) Suffragettes were women in the UK	iii) have to gain formal nomination as candidates.
d) Jamaica	iv) was granted full adult suffrage in 1944.
e) In most democracies today	v) was not given to all adults.
f) Citizens who want to stand for election	vi) who fought for the right to vote.
g) In order to cast a vote,	vii) behind closed doors.
h) When a voter is marking their ballot paper,	viii) in a ballot box.
i) Secret ballots allow people	ix) nobody should watch them.
j) Voters put their ballot papers	x) so that people cannot tamper with them.
k) Ballot boxes are sealed	xi) the voter makes a cross against the name of a candidate.
l) The ballot boxes are opened	xii) to vote freely with no intimidation from others.

5 You have been asked by a visitor about how a person qualifies to vote in an election, and also how a person qualifies to be candidate in an election in Jamaica. Outline what you will explain to this visitor about an elector and a candidate in a Jamaican election.

_____

_____

_____

_____

_____

_____

_____

_____

_____

6 Use your phone or tablet to find the full results of a recent election (local or national). Present the results as a) a pie diagram and b) as a bar graph. On a separate sheet, explain which diagram best represents the information?

7 **Read pages 176–9 of the student book. Then answer the following questions.**

a) What is a floating voter?

_____

b) What does a candidate have to achieve to win in a first-past-the-post system?

_____

c) How often do elections have to be held?

_____

d) Under what circumstances can the Prime Minister, Premier or President, or Chief Minister call for early elections?

_____

_____

e) When are the results of an election announced?

_____

f) What is the main role of the Electoral Commission of Jamaica (ECJ)?

_____

g) What is a hung parliament?

_____

_____

h) What do candidates and political parties do first after Nomination Day?

_____

i) What typically happens during an election campaign?

_____

j) What does the Political Ombudsman do?

_____

_____

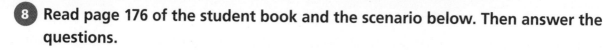

8 Read page 176 of the student book and the scenario below. Then answer the questions.

Butterfly Island is divided into five constituencies. There are two main political parties which represent the people of Butterfly Island, the BSP and TNP. Butterfly Island uses the first-past-the-post electoral system. The table below shows the results of the 2021 elections.

Constituency	Number of persons who voted	No. of votes received (BSP)	No. of votes received (TNP)
1	3000	2500	500
2	2500	900	1600
3	2500	1000	1500
4	3000	1400	1600
5	2000	1500	500
Total	13000	7300	5700

a) What is the total number of persons who voted in the election? _____

b) Which political party received the majority of the votes? _____

c) Which political party won the seats for three or more of the constituencies?

_____

d) Which political party will form the new government for Butterfly Island? Explain the reason for this. _____

_____

e) Outline at least one advantage and one disadvantage of this electoral system.

_____

_____

f) If Butterfly Island were to adopt the proportional representation electoral system, which party would have formed the government? Explain why.

_____

_____

9 Read pages 180–1 of the student book, 'The process on election day'. Then number the following procedures from 1 to 11 in the order they take place in the voting process on election day in Jamaica.

a) After counting, the results are announced by the returning officer. _____

b) At the end of the voting period, the ballot boxes are taken to a central place in the constituency. _____

c) The ballots are counted. _____

d) The empty ballot boxes are displayed by the presiding officer to prove they are empty. _____

e) The presiding officer locks and seals the ballot boxes. _____

f) The presiding officer or polling clerk checks the names against the voter list. _____

g) The voter folds the completed ballot paper and puts it in the ballot box. _____

h) The voter goes to a private voting booth. _____

i) The voter makes a 'X' next to the candidate they wish to vote for. _____

j) The voter receives an official ballot paper with an official mark. _____

k) Voters give their names to the presiding officer or a polling clerk. _____

10 Imagine you have just voted in an election. Write an explanation for a younger brother or sister of exactly what you did.

Include where and when you voted / what you took with you / what you did at the polling station / how you felt after voting / what you are waiting for now.

_____

_____

_____

_____

_____

_____

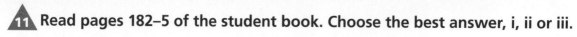
11 **Read pages 182–5 of the student book. Choose the best answer, i, ii or iii.**

a) Candidates who get the most votes in a constituency:

   i) become members of the government.

   ii) become members of the House of Representatives.

   iii) become ministers or junior ministers.

b) Cabinet members are appointed by:

   i) the electorate.

   ii) the House of Representatives.

   iii) the Prime Minister.

c) The Opposition is formed from:

   i) the largest party in the House of Representatives.

   ii) the second largest party in the House of Representatives.

   iii) all the parties who are not in the government.

d) Women in Jamaica got full adult suffrage in:

   i) 1830   **ii)** 1920   **iii)** 1944

e) An election is **not** free and fair if:

   i) there is intimidation of voters.

   ii) there is universal adult suffrage.

   iii) there is freedom of speech during the election.

f) When talking about elections, **transparent** means:

   i) with no intimidation or bribery.

   ii) free for people of all races, genders, beliefs, etc. to take part in.

   iii) open and done in a way without any secrets.

g) CAFFE is:

   i) a political party.   **ii)** an election watchdog.

   iii) an organisation to promote patriotism.

Complete this quiz about the whole of Unit 6. Look back at the photographs and *Did you know ...?* boxes as well as the text in the student book.

12 Answer these questions.

a) What date was the general election in 2020?

_____

b) Why do people get a red mark on a finger after they vote?

_____

c) How many political constituencies are there in Jamaica?

_____

d) On what date did Jamaica get full adult suffrage?

_____

e) What or who were suffragettes?

_____

f) Why are ballot boxes sealed?

_____

g) Why do you think voting in most countries is done using a secret ballot?

_____

h) Why do you think political parties try to win the votes of floating voters?

_____

i) If an election results in a hung parliament, what can the politicians do?

_____

j) Why do the police go to polling stations during elections?

_____

k) Why should voters fold their ballot papers after making their choice?

_____

13 **Explain the roles of the following:**

a) An election candidate: _____

_____

b) The Electoral Commission of Jamaica _____

_____

c) The Office of the Political Ombudsman _____

_____

d) A returning officer _____

_____

e) A presiding officer _____

_____

f) A poll clerk _____

_____

14 **Imagine you are running for class president. Write your election manifesto.**

_____

_____

_____

_____

_____

_____

_____

_____

_____

1 Read pages 194–5 of the student book, 'Preservation and conservation of the environment'. Unscramble the key vocabulary and then match the words to their definition.

a) ritvonpeeras _____

b) sinnaerovtoc _____

c) taisiyatsbluni _____

d) snarleougti _____

e) perdcetot _____

f) ptrioihdbe _____

g) rctsunyaa _____

h) adstrienoetof _____

i) _____ A place where people or animals that are in danger can go to be safe.

ii) _____ Rules made by a government or other authority to control the way people behave.

iii) _____ Something that is not allowed by order.

iv) _____ Something that the law does not allow to be destroyed or damaged.

v) _____ The ability to be maintained at a steady level without using up all the natural resources or causing environmental damage.

vi) _____ The act of keeping something as it is or protecting it from harm.

vii) _____ The act of saving and protecting the environment.

viii) _____ The cutting down of trees in a large area, or the destruction of forests by people.

2 Write sentences of your own using the eight words from activity 1.

_____

_____

_____

_____

_____

_____

_____

3 Read pages 196–7 of the student book, 'What is green technology?'. Complete the diagram to summarise the benefits of green technology.

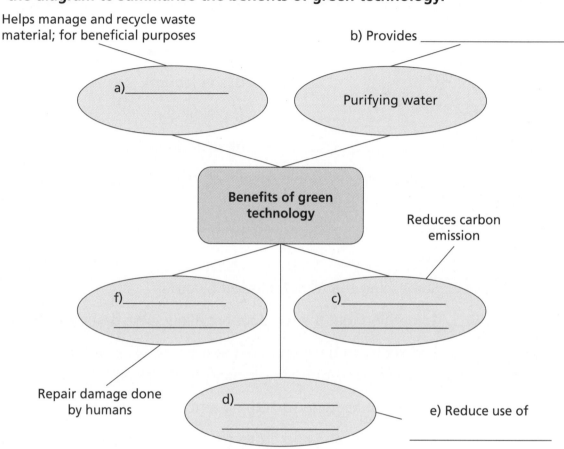

Helps manage and recycle waste material; for beneficial purposes

a) _____

b) Provides _____

Purifying water

Benefits of green technology

Reduces carbon emission

f) _____ _____

c) _____ _____

Repair damage done by humans

d) _____ _____

e) Reduce use of _____

4 Write a paragraph about green technology in Jamaica.

_____

_____

_____

_____

_____

_____

_____

_____

_____

5 Read pages 198–205 of the student book. 'Types of green technology and how they are used in Jamaica'. Complete each of the following key points about recycling.

Why you should recycle.

a) Recycling reduces _____

_____

b) Recycling conserves _____

_____

c) Recycling helps to reduce _____

_____

d) Recycling materials uses less _____

_____

e) Recycling helps conserve _____

_____

How you can recycle.

f) Use _____

_____

g) Don't throw _____

_____

h) Use recyclable _____

_____

i) Cut down on the use of _____

_____

j) Give away _____

_____

6 Complete the diagram to summarise Jamaica's main water resources and how green technology is, or could be applied in treating them.

Surface water	Water from _____ _____	is treated _____ _____
Desalination	Water from _____ _____	is treated _____ _____
Groundwater	Water from _____ _____	is treated _____ _____

7 Explain the meaning of these key terms.

a) Fuel-efficient cars _____

_____

b) Human-induced CO_2 emissions _____

_____

c) Fossil fuels _____

_____

d) Waste by-products _____

_____

e) Energy-saving light bulbs _____

_____

f) Global energy needs _____

_____

g) A renewable source of energy _____

_____

8 Summarise the advantages and disadvantages of the three forms of green technology.

Advantages	Disadvantages
Solar power	
Wind power	
Hydroelectric power	

9 Find 14 words, or pairs of words, from pages 198–205 in the puzzle below.

```
R P U R I F I C A T I O N A C X L E W N
E L Q N M D B R P Q Y Q L H A O A N Y M
C A F O S S I L F U E L O Y R K M E A V
Y A E O F B G B W R P I G U B K R R W G
C V H L C R L O H R J F H L O U F G W E
L C H B O Q X Z S R K K O A N I G Y N N
I Z F R I Z E C Y N I Q Q C D G W E E E
N A C E Q Q Z Q S S N V C M I P V F V R
G X K N T Z S D R Z E W H X O A W F W A
Q T D E S A L I N A T I O N X H B I I T
I M K W J U G Q U C I Q Z Z I M Q C N E
G G K A I V H U O E C H N J D M X I D K
H W P B O V J O A M E X V A E V T E T K
R E D L Q R P C E K N R A E O L E N U Y
S T X E F H P P F W E E H U K O Y C R M
J Y M R J C A N F I R I Z G R I D Y B B
F I S F E R W D T V G Y Q R V Q D Y I Y
A V I A T I O N J Y Y S Q J H D W F N I
E E O C A R B O N E M I S S I O N S E Z
H Y D R O E L E C T R I C W D A X L J Y
```

Horizontal words	Vertical words

10 Read pages 206–7 of the student book, 'Green technology in businesses'. Are these sentences true or false?

a) Gary Hendrickson is the Chief Technical Officer of the National Baking Company with responsibility for green technology.   *True/False*

b) Solar-powered lamps are used everywhere at the National Baking Company. *True/False*

c) Propane is used in all the ovens.   *True/False*

d) Biodiesel fuel is made from leftover cooking oil.   *True/False*

e) The National Baking Company's trucks use only biodiesel fuel.   *True/False*

f) The National Baking Company has been using biodiesel since 2007.   *True/False*

g) Precautions have been taken to avoid biofuel pollution.   *True/False*

h) Bags for bread and rolls are not made from plastic.   *True/False*

i) The 'polluter pays' principle is a regulation making those who pollute pay to manage the pollution and prevent damage to people or the environment. *True/False*

j) The Rockfort Power Station will be the first desalination plant in Jamaica. *True/False*

k) The Rockfort Power Station will cost $35 000 to build.   *True/False*

l) Shelly-Ann discussed the costs of poultry farming in Jamaica at an international conference.   *True/False*

11 Rewrite the false sentences from activity 10 as true sentences.

_____

_____

_____

_____

_____

_____

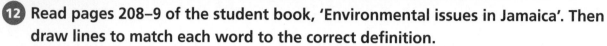
12 Read pages 208–9 of the student book, 'Environmental issues in Jamaica'. Then draw lines to match each word to the correct definition.

a) endangered		**i)**	A group of plants or animals whose members have the same main characteristics
b) species		**ii)**	A wide variety of animal and plant species living in their natural environment
c) endemic		**iii)**	All the animals and plants that live together in a particular area with a relationship between them and their environment
d) extinction		**iv)**	Become less in quantity, importance or strength
e) monitored		**v)**	Doing something without meaning to or realising what is happening
f) decline		**vi)**	In danger: usually describing animals that there are very few of and that are close to extinction
g) degradation		**vii)**	Regularly checked
h) inadvertently		**viii)**	Something that breaks down naturally so can be thrown away without causing pollution
i) biodegradable		**ix)**	Something that is naturally present in an area
j) invasive		**x)**	Something which comes from a different region and spreads very quickly causing a problem
k) biodiversity		**xi)**	The illegal hunting or killing of animals without the landowner's permission
l) ecosystem		**xii)**	The process in which something becomes worse or weaker
m) offset		**xiii)**	To do something to reduce the impact or harm of something else that has been done
n) poaching		**xiv)**	When all members of an animal or plant species dies out

13 Read pages 210–11 of the student book, 'Deforestation'. Then draw lines to join the beginnings of the sentences with the correct ending.

a)	Forests are made up of	**i)**	a home for animals and plants.
b)	Forests act	**ii)**	a source of fuel and building materials.
c)	Forest provide	**iii)**	as a watershed capturing rainfall into aquifers.
d)	Trees produce	**iv)**	carbon dioxide from the air.
e)	Forests extract	**v)**	natural ecosystems with many important functions.
f)	Forests are	**vi)**	oxygen which we need to survive.
g)	Bauxite mining requires	**vii)**	greater production of food and goods which requires clearing of forest.
h)	Tourism requires	**viii)**	major damage to trees and forests.
i)	Population growth leads to	**ix)**	the construction of resorts and infrastructure which results in deforestation.
j)	Hurricanes cause	**x)**	the removal of vegetation and topsoil, and also the building roads into the forests.
k)	Deforestation causes	**xi)**	encourage and involve the people in forest conservation.
l)	Watercourses become	**xii)**	full of sediment so water flows decrease leading to water shortages and floods.
m)	The Forest Policy for Jamaica (2015) aims	**xiii)**	soil erosion and a decline in the quality of agricultural land.
n)	The 2015 Forest Policy commits to	**xiv)**	to reduce deforestation.

14 Read pages 212–15 of the student book, 'Pollution and land degradation'. Then write possible clues for this crossword on this and the next page.

Across

3. _____

_____

4. _____

_____

7. _____

_____

10. _____

_____

12. _____

_____

13. _____

_____

14. _____

_____

Down

1. _____

_____

2. _____

_____

5. _____

_____

6. _____

_____

8. _____

_____

9. _____

_____

11. _____

_____

15 **Read pages 216–17 of the student book, 'Sea levels rising'. Then answer these questions.**

a) What are the two major causes of sea level rise?

i) _____

ii) _____

b) What are the three main effects of sea temperature rise in Jamaica?

i) _____

ii) _____

iii) _____

c) What are three possible solutions to rising water levels?

i) _____

ii) _____

iii) _____

16 **Think about your personal response to some of the issues raised in this unit and make notes.**

a) What I already do to reduce my carbon footprint.

_____

_____

_____

_____

b) What I could do to reduce my carbon footprint in the future.

_____

_____

_____

_____

1 **Read pages 224–31 of the student book. Then unscramble the word/words below and match the correct letter to each definition.**

a) p l u m m e t o n n e y   **b)** s q u i l i f t a c i a n o   **c)** f l e s - s m e e t e

d) e c h o i c   **e)** s t a w n   **f)** d r a n s d a t f o g l i n v i

g) g n e w d o k l e   **h)** r e c a r e   **i)** l i l s k s

j) s e n d e   **k)** i e c s e e n p r t s e   **l)** y t h m a p e

i) How you feel about yourself _____

ii) The understanding someone has about a particular subject _____

_____

iii) The act of choosing or selecting _____

iv) Things that are essential for everyday living _____

v) When someone does not have a job _____

vi) Something, such as degrees or diplomas, that you get when you successfully finish a course of study _____

vii) Items that a person would like to have, but are not essential for everyday life or basic survival _____

viii) The ability to share another person's feelings and emotions as if they were your own _____

ix) The level of comfort and wealth that a person or family may have

_____

x) A person's long-term path in a job or occupation _____

xi) The knowledge or ability to do something well _____

xii) The ability to keep going and make continuing effort even when it is difficult

_____

2 **Conduct a short survey of ten adults to find out the main reason they work and do the jobs they do.**

- Make copies of the form below and give one to each adult.
- Ask the adults to tick those that apply to them.
- Examine all the answers and show the results using a bar graph in the space below.

Why do you work and do the job that you now do? Instruction: Tick all the factors that apply to you.	
To take care of my basic needs and work towards my dreams.	
It is my passion; it is what I have always wanted to do.	
It allows me to use my talents and earn from them.	
It allows me to give back to my community while making a living.	
My family is dependent on me so I have to work.	
It is a way of building my skills and experience to advance my career.	
It is not my chosen career but it meets my needs for now.	
I enjoy helping people and this job allows me to do that.	

3 Read pages 232–3 of the student book, 'The hotel industry'. Then answer the questions.

a) What does a hotelier do? _____

b) Some hotels have managers for different departments. Explain why they do this.

_____

c) What do events planners organise?

i) _____   ii) _____

iii) _____   iv) _____

d) What are the functions of the marketing staff in a hotel?

_____

e) What are the main duties of the housekeeping staff?

_____

f) Apart from welcoming new guests, what else do reception staff do?

i) _____

ii) _____

g) Who may the kitchen staff include?

i) _____   ii) _____

iii) _____   iv) _____

v) _____

h) What do tour guides do? _____

_____

i) What does a caterer organise with a client?

i) _____

ii) _____

j) Not all careers in the hotel industry involve working in a hotel. The hotel industry has links with other industries. Make a list of five other careers that are connected to the hotel industry and briefly describe the connection. Use a separate sheet of paper.

4 **Read pages 234–5 of the student book, 'Personal development'. Then answer the questions.**

a) What are five key elements that people tend to bring to their work or contribute to a job?

i) _____   ii) _____

iii) _____   iv) _____

v) _____

b) What is the difference between knowledge and a skill? Give an example of each.

_____

_____

_____

c) Practice and experience are two ways in which we can develop our skills. How can a young person practise and gain experience before joining the workforce?

_____

_____

_____

d) Explain why personal qualities and potential should be considered along with academic abilities when deciding on a career.

_____

_____

_____

_____

e) Select any two institutions that offer training after graduating from secondary school in Jamaica. For each one, write a brief overview of the type of institution, what programmes they offer and what qualifications are necessary for enrolment. Use a separate sheet of paper.

5 Read pages 234–39 of the student book. Use the word bank and add them in the correct place in the diagrams.

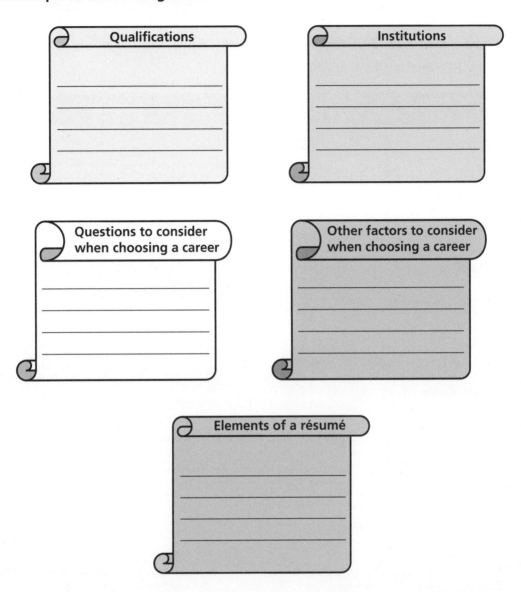

Qualifications

_____
_____
_____
_____

Institutions

_____
_____
_____
_____

Questions to consider when choosing a career

_____
_____
_____
_____

Other factors to consider when choosing a career

_____
_____
_____
_____

Elements of a résumé

_____
_____
_____
_____

cooperation	shift work	references	needs and wants
experience	values and attitudes		opportunities for promotion
teacher training college	curriculum	hobbies	health issues
universities	problem solving		contact information
potential	nursing college	passion	talents

6 Read pages 240–3 of the student book, 'Applying for a job'. Then think of your ideal job and write the job description.

Job Opportunity

Company name: _____

Type of job: _____

Position: _____

Location: _____

Job summary

_____

_____

_____

Job responsibilities

_____

_____

_____

Job requirements

Essential: _____

_____

_____

_____

Desirable: _____

_____

_____

_____

7 Read pages 238–47 of the student book. Then use the word bank to complete the sentences.

a) A _____ should include key information, plus a summary of what you can offer the employer.

b) He is a distinguished _____, who used to attend this school.

c) The new science teacher uses very _____ methods to make the subject interesting.

d) Some _____ require people to work hard to show politeness, professionalism and to develop a sense of connection to each other.

e) The _____ of an office means that workers can get into conflicts with colleagues.

f) Some work friendships develop into an _____, though most employers discourage this.

g) Having _____ at work can badly damage the cohesion of the group and can reduce the job satisfaction of the people involved.

h) It's always best to be friendly, professional and _____ towards your work colleagues.

i) It is important to _____ clearly and politely with your co-workers, answer all letters and emails and return calls.

j) Workers have to _____ and should always try to carry through with what they said they would do.

k) Marianne complained about a co-worker after he had made _____ remarks to her.

l) It is essential that you understand your _____ when you start work in a company, and do your best to fulfil it.

intimate relationship	scholar	communicate	résumé
enemies suggestive	take responsibility	respectful	role
hierarchy	workplace relationships	innovative	

8 Read the job advertisement for a customer service professional on pages 240–1 of the student book. Mary-Anne fully qualifies for the job. Write her resume below to apply for the post.

_____

_____

_____

_____

_____

_____

_____

_____

9 Mary-Anne has received a call from the company and has been invited to attend an interview. Write a list of questions she should expect to be asked by the interview panel.

_____

_____

_____

_____

_____

_____

_____

_____

_____

10 Read pages 246–7 of the student book, 'Problems in the workplace'. Match the words in the word bank to the correct definition.

a) Behaviour towards someone of a flirting or sexual nature that the person has not encouraged. _____

b) A statement with a possible second meaning, usually something unpleasant and often referring to sex. _____

c) Something given that was not asked for and usually not wanted.

_____

d) Remarks that make people think of sex in a way that makes them feel uncomfortable. _____

e) Offensive in a sexual way. _____

f) Not suitable for a particular situation or purpose. _____

unsolicited	sexual harassment	obscene
innuendo	suggestive comments	inappropriate

11 What do you expect from a job in the future? In about 250 words, write what is important or unimportant to you about your future career. Think about:

- the salary
- working hours
- flexible working hours
- working from home
- friendly colleagues
- any of your own ideas.

- annual increase in salary
- sexual harassment rules
- dangerous conditions
- continuous training
- chances of promotion

_____

_____

_____

_____

_____

_____

_____

_____

_____

12 Read pages 248–51 of the student book. Draw lines to match the key vocabulary to the correct definitions.

a)	duty of care	**i)**	A fault or failing in a thing or person
b)	redundancy	**ii)**	A process of assessing the strengths and weaknesses of a person when doing their job
c)	termination	**iii)**	A time or date by which a task must be finished
d)	defect	**iv)**	Achieved, or done well at
e)	accomplished	**v)**	An accurate and deep understanding of something
f)	appraisal	**vi)**	Items that protect someone from danger or injury
g)	aspirations	**vii)**	The desires of a person to do or achieve something
h)	insight	**viii)**	The end of something in time or space
i)	protective equipment	**ix)**	The legal requirement to keep someone from harm when they are in your care
j)	deadline	**x)**	When a job is ended by the employer and the employee has to leave the employment

13 Which basic workers' rights are the following scenarios talking about?

a) 'You've been working here for more than three years so you will be paid while you are away having your baby.' _____

b) 'This is dangerous: we shouldn't have to do this work without protective clothing or equipment!' _____

c) 'If the company does close, they'll have to tell us and pay us at least a few months' wages.' _____

d) 'I think we should be getting more money next month: the government has said everyone in this type of job will get an increase.'

_____

e) 'If you are ill, the company will have to continue paying your wages while you are getting better.' _____

14 Read pages 252–5 of the student book. Answer the following questions about the workplace.

a) If someone has a grievance against another employee, what does a company normally start?

i) Internal procedures

ii) Informal discussions

iii) Independent decisions

iv) Impartial solutions

b) If a dispute between employers and employees cannot be settled, and the employees are members of a trade union, who can mediate?

i) The local magistrates court

ii) The government

iii) An independent court

iv) The trade union

c) What is the main function of a trade union?

i) Building solidarity

ii) It looks after its members

iii) Collective bargaining

iv) Housing assistance

d) What is it called when workers deliberately reduce their work rate?

i) Work to rule

ii) Go on strike

iii) Stay away from work

iv) Go slow

Are these statements true or false?

e) Collective bargaining is done on behalf of all of a trade union's members.
True/False

f) Being a member of a trade union can help provide job security.
True/False

g) The Bustamente Industrial Trade Union had a membership of 54 000 by 1942.
True/False

h) The aims of the Caribbean Union of Teachers (CUT) include raising concerns about health and safety of teachers and students in schools.
True/False

15 **Complete the words using the clues given.**

a) A disagreement between workers and their employer

__ __ __ u __ __ __ i __ __   __ __ __ __ __ __ e

b) Organisations of working people, such as trade unions, that campaign for better conditions

__ a__ __ __ __   __ o__ e __ __ __ __

c) When workers do just enough work so they are within the terms of their job role or contract

__ o __ __   __ __   __ u __ __

d) Discussions between employers and trade unions about pay and working conditions

__ __ __ __ e__ __ __ __ e   __ a __ __ a __ __ __ __ __

e) Try to end a disagreement between two people or groups

__ __ __ i __ __ __

f) State formally that you are leaving a job permanently

__ __ s __ __ __

g) When workers do not work as fast as usual

__ __   __ __ o __

h) An organisation of workers that aims to improve pay and conditions for its members

__ r __ __ __   __ __ i __ __

16 **Read the following scenario and present relevant arguments.**

Mr Plummer has worked at Brash Industries for years but has never considered joining a trade union. He is worried that his salary is not adequate enough to spare even a small amount to cover the membership fees. However, his co-workers are trying to convince him of the benefits of joining a union. Outline some of the arguments his co-workers may use to convince him to join. Use a separate sheet of paper.

1 Read pages 262–3 of the student book, 'Tourism in Jamaica'. Write the examples of holiday activities in the correct box.

deep sea fishing	hiking	water sports	bamboo rafting
visiting unspoilt areas		meeting local people	
learning local cooking	golf	understanding local culture	

Mass tourism	Ecotourism	Community tourism

2 Draw the symbols and name five points of interest and five major resorts on the map. Complete your map with an appropriate title.

Key
- ■ National park
- ★ Point of interest
- ■ Major resort

Scale 1 : 1 250 000

3 Choose one point of interest on your map and explain the type of tourism it could be associated with and why tourists will find it worth visiting.

_____

_____

_____

_____

4 Read pages 264–5 of the student book, 'Development of the tourist industry'. Write the headings in the correct place above the examples of natural factors affecting tourism.

climate	fauna	flora	natural sites

a) _____	b) _____	c) _____	d) _____
coral reefs	light rainfall	coastal mangroves	turtles
lagoons	moderate winds	rainforests	rare birds
waterfalls	warm temperatures	varied vegetation	reef fish

5 Tick the activities which are popular with tourists in Jamaica.

a) bird watching ☐   b) exploring natural sites ☐   c) snowboarding ☐

d) fishing ☐   e) golf ☐   f) hiking ☐

g) reef diving ☐   h) skydiving ☐   i) snorkelling ☐

6 Write a sentence about each activity you ticked above to explain why tourists visit Jamaica to enjoy it.

_____

_____

_____

_____

_____

_____

7 Coral reefs play an important role in the natural environment. Conduct research to find out the following about coral reefs. Use a separate sheet of paper.

a) What are corals?

b) How do corals support fish and other aquatic life?

c) How do corals help in the formation and protection of beaches?

8 Read pages 266–7 of the student book, 'Tourism and culture'. Unscramble the words relating to tourism and culture below.

i) i e n i s e m a t _____

ii) c r a u y n l i _____

iii) l a s e v f s t i _____

iv) l t i a h o t s p i y _____

v) n o e u i g s i d n _____

vi) i n i e r n e d s g t _____

vii) t o P s a i _____

viii) t e b a l s _____

9 Use the words above to complete the sentences.

Tourists are far more likely to visit (a) _____ countries such as Jamaica, that have not suffered wars or serious social unrest. They want to enjoy some luxury and comfort on their holiday and so expect the same (b) _____ that they have at home. They certainly do not appreciate shortages of water or electricity.

Many tourists are interested in the unique cultural features of a country, whether that is the environment, the buildings, the (c) _____ arts and crafts or the lives of the people. In Jamaica we have a rich cultural heritage which also includes the language we speak – our (d) _____ which has developed from a mix of many different sources.

Visitors from overseas often wish to explore all aspects of a culture, including the (e) _____ aspect. Most will wish to taste local dishes but some may like to go further and join courses to learn to cook using local (f) _____.

Tourists love to think they can make friends when they visit another country so the (g) _____ of the people is very important. Jamaican people understand this and make visitors comfortable. They can also welcome visitors to an exciting range of music and dance (h) _____ where visitors can mix with local people.

10 Read pages 268–9 of the student book, 'Advantages of tourism'. Are these sentences true or false?

a) Fewer tourists visited Jamaica in 2016 than 2017. *True/False*

b) More tourists visited Jamaica in 2007 than 2006. *True/False*

c) About 25% of jobs in Jamaica are in tourism. *True/False*

d) In the first half of 2019, Jamaica received US$3.3 billion from tourism. *True/False*

e) In 2018, 4.32 million tourists visited Jamaica. *True/False*

f) Tourism indirectly creates jobs in the transport, tour and craft sectors. *True/False*

11 Rewrite the false sentences as true sentences.

_____

_____

_____

12 Draw lines to match the words or phrases to their meanings.

a) revenue

i) Money that a person or organisation gets for doing a job

b) earnings

ii) The services and facilities that allow a country to work properly, e.g. transport, energy supply

c) interconnectedness

iii) The amount of money people have to spend and to buy things

d) infrastructure

iv) When countries or organisations are connected to each other

e) multiplier effect

v) Money that a government or business receives from people

f) spending power

vi) The way more and more money can be produced in the economy of a country

13 Read pages 270–1 of the student book, 'Cruise tourism'. Complete the table to compare cruise tourism and long-stay tourism.

		Cruise tourism	Long-stay tourism
a)	Duration of stay	1 or 2 days	
b)	Spend money		All on one island
c)	Benefit to		One island
d)	Activities	Participate in one only, plus shopping	
e)	Location of visits		Have the time to travel more widely

14 Complete the sentences with words from the text.

Cruise tourism:

a) provides _____ for Jamaicans, and provides training and skills development.

b) provides guaranteed customers and _____ for tour companies.

c) brings large numbers of tourists which _____ local businesses.

d) pays a _____ which goes to the government.

e) provides _____ for Caribbean tourism.

15 Answer the questions about the information in the graphs.

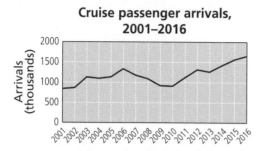

Cruise passenger arrivals, 2001–2016

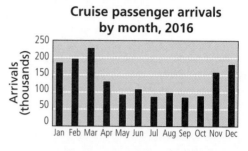

Cruise passenger arrivals by month, 2016

a) Which sentence describes the information in the first graph best?

i)   There was a gradual increase in passenger arrivals between 2001 and 2016.

ii) There was a gradual increase between 2001 and 2016 apart from a dip in 2009 and 2010.

iii) There was a gradual increase from 2001 to 2006 followed by a gradual decline for four years before a further increase up to 2016.

b) Study the second graph.

i) Which is the busiest month for tourism? _____

ii) Which is the quietest month? _____

16 Read pages 268–9 and 272–3 of the student book. Use the word bank to complete the advantages and disadvantages of tourism in Jamaica

Advantages of tourism	Disadvantages of tourism
_____	_____
_____	_____
_____	_____
_____	_____

better standard of living   higher national income   land degradation

improved services and infrastructure   loss of farmland and communal areas

pollution   job creation   water shortages

17 Write a paragraph on the advantages of tourism for Jamaica and another on the disadvantages. Use a separate sheet of paper.

18 Write a paragraph on what you think the government and tourist industry in Jamaica can do in order to reduce the impact of tourism on the environment.

_____

_____

_____

_____

_____

_____

_____

19 Complete the crossword. Use vocabulary in unit 9.

Across

3. Useful or pleasant facilities in a place

7. Harmful or poisonous substances put into the environment

9. A place where a ship stops during a journey (4, 2, 4)

10. A tax on each person doing something, often entering a country (4, 3)

11. A place where a lot of people go for a holiday

14. The traditions and features of life that have continued over many years in a country or region and have been passed on from one generation to another

15. A geographical term referring to how countries are connected in the modern world

16. The natural environment in which a plant or animal lives

Down

1. A friendly, welcoming behaviour towards visitors or guests

2. Holiday and related services which do no harm to the environment or local culture

4. A description of the way income can generate further income for a country (10, 6)

5. The port or harbour where is ship is based (4, 4)

6. All the plant life of a particular place

8. The process in which the quality of something is reduced

12. All the animal life of a particular place

13. The gradual destruction of the soil or rocks in a place, usually by water or wind

20 Identify an activity or site in your community that could be promoted as a tourist attraction. Use your cell phone or tablet to do a three-minute video to promote the activity or site as an attraction for tourists. The video should include the use of original music, poetry or speech.